# GEMINI

_SUN SIGN SERIES_

FLBurr

This book
    belongs
      to :

FLBurr

August 11th, 2012

ALSO BY JOANNA MARTINE WOOLFOLK

*Sexual Astrology*

*Honeymoon for Life*

*The Only Astrology Book You'll Ever Need*

# GEMINI

## SUN SIGN SERIES
# JOANNA MARTINE WOOLFOLK

**TAYLOR TRADE PUBLISHING**
LANHAM • NEW YORK • BOULDER • TORONTO • PLYMOUTH, UK

Published by Taylor Trade Publishing
An imprint of The Rowman & Littlefield Publishing Group, Inc.
4501 Forbes Boulevard, Suite 200, Lanham, Maryland 20706
www.rlpgtrade.com

Estover Road, Plymouth PL6 7PY, United Kingdom

Distributed by National Book Network

British Library Cataloguing in Publication Information Available

**Library of Congress Cataloging-in-Publication Data**

Woolfolk, Joanna Martine.
　Gemini / Joanna Martine Woolfolk.
　　p. cm.—(Sun sign series)
　ISBN 978-1-58979-555-6 (pbk. : alk. paper)—ISBN 978-1-58979-530-3 (electronic)
　1. Gemini (Astrology) I. Title.
　BF1727.25.W66 2011
　133.5'264—dc22　　　　　　　　　　　　　　　　2011003094

♾ ™　The paper used in this publication meets the minimum requirements of American
National Standard for Information Sciences—Permanence of Paper for Printed Library
Materials, ANSI/NISO Z39.48-1992.

Printed in the United States of America

*I dedicate this book to the memory of*
*William Woolfolk*
*whose wisdom continues to guide me,*

*and to*
*James Sgandurra*
*who made everything bloom again.*

# CONTENTS

# ABOUT THE AUTHOR

Astrologer Joanna Martine Woolfolk has had a long career as an author, columnist, lecturer, and counselor. She has written the monthly horoscope for numerous magazines in the United States, Europe, and Latin America—among them *Marie Claire*, *Harper's Bazaar*, *Redbook*, *Self*, *YM*, *House Beautiful*, and *StarScroll International*. In addition to the best-selling *The Only Astrology Book You'll Ever Need*, Joanna is the author of *Sexual Astrology*, which has sold over a million copies worldwide, and *Astrology Source*, an interactive CD-ROM.

Joanna is a popular television and radio personality who has been interviewed by Barbara Walters, Regis Philbin, and Sally Jessy Raphael. She has appeared in a regular astrology segment on *New York Today* on NBC-TV and on *The Fairfield Exchange* on

CT Cable Channel 12, and she appears frequently on television and radio shows around the country. You can visit her website at www.joannamartinewoolfolk.com.

# ACKNOWLEDGMENTS

Many people contribute to the creation of a book, some with ideas and editorial suggestions, and some unknowingly through their caring and love.

Among those who must know how much they helped is Jed Lyons, the elegant, erudite president of my publishers, the Rowman & Littlefield Publishing Group. Jed gave me the idea for this Sun Sign series, and I am grateful for his faith and encouragement.

Enormous gratitude also to Michael K. Dorr, my literary agent and dear friend, who has believed in me since we first met and continues to be my champion. I thank Michael for his sharp editor's eye and imbuing me with confidence.

Two people who don't know how much they give are my beloved sister and brother, Patricia G. Reynhout and Dr. John T. Galdamez. They sustain me with their unfailing devotion and support.

*We are born at a given moment, in a given place,
and like vintage years of wine, we have the
qualities of the year and of the season
in which we are born.*

CARL GUSTAV JUNG

# INTRODUCTION

When my publishers suggested I write a book devoted solely to Gemini, I was thrilled. I've long wanted to concentrate exclusively on your wonderful sign. You are very special in the zodiac. Astrology teaches that Gemini is the sign most quintessentially *human*. Gemini represents communication, mental agility, and dexterity, as well as an ability to envision complicated concepts and solve problems—and to leave a written record. These are all qualities that set human beings apart from the rest of the animal kingdom. Gemini also does not have an animal as its symbol. Your sign is symbolized by a pair of human twins. Karmic teachers say you were specially picked to be a Gemini because of your passion for knowledge and spirit of exploration in your previous life. But whether or not one believes in past lives, in *this* life you are Gemini, the great communicator.

These days it has become fashionable to be a bit dismissive of Sun signs (the sign that the Sun was in at the time of your birth). Some people sniff that "everyone knows about Sun signs." They say the descriptions are too "cookie-cutter," too much like cardboard figures, too inclusive (how can every Gemini be the same?).

Of course every Gemini is not the same! And many of these differences are not only genetic and environmental, but are differences in your *charts*. Another Gemini would not necessarily have your Moon sign, or Venus sign, or Ascendant. However, these are factors to consider later—after you have studied your Sun sign. (In *The Only Astrology Book You'll Ever Need*, I cover in depth differences in charts: different Planets, Houses, Ascendants, etc.)

First and foremost, you are a Gemini. This is the sign the Sun was traveling through at the time of your birth.* The Sun is our most powerful planet. (In astrological terms, the Sun is referred to as a planet even though technically it is a "luminary.") It gives us life, warmth, energy, and food. It is the force that sustains us on Earth. The Sun is also the most important and pervasive influence in your horoscope and in many ways determines how others see you. Your Sun sign governs your individuality, your distinctive style, and your drive to fulfill your goals.

Your sign of Gemini symbolizes the role you are given to play in this life. It's as if at the moment of your birth you were pushed onstage into a drama called *This Is My Life*. In this drama, you are the starring actor—and Gemini is the character you play. What aspects of this character are you going to project? The Gemini curiosity and expressiveness? Its enthusiasm for learning and daring intelligence? Or its cynicism and tricky manipulation? Your sign of Gemini describes your journey through this life, for it is your task to evolve into a perfect Gemini.

For each of us, the most interesting, most gripping subject is *self*. The longer I am an astrologer—which at this point is half my lifetime—the more I realize that what we all want to know about

*From our viewpoint here on Earth, the Sun travels around the Earth once each year. Within the space of that year the Sun moves through all twelve signs of the zodiac, spending approximately one month in each sign.

is ourselves. "Who am I?" you ask. You want to know what makes you tick, why you have such intense feelings, and whether others are also insecure. People ask me questions like "What kind of man should I look for?" "Why am I discontented with my job?" or "The woman I'm dating is a Scorpio; will we be happy together?" They ask me if they'll ever find true love and when they will get out of a period of sadness or fear or the heavy burden of problems. They ask about their path in life and how they can find more fulfillment.

So I continue to see that the reason astrology exists is to answer questions about you. Basically, it's all about *you*. Astrology has been described as a stairway leading into your deeper self. It holds out the promise that you do not have to pass through life reacting blindly to experience, that you can, within limits, direct your own destiny and in the process reach a truer self-understanding.

Astrologically, the place to begin the study of yourself is your Sun sign. In this book, you'll read about your many positive qualities as well as your Gemini issues and negative inclinations. You'll find insights into your power and potentials, advice about love and sex, career guidance, health and diet tips, and information about myriads of objects, places, concepts, and things to which Gemini is attached. You'll also find topics not usually included in other astrology books—such as how Gemini fits in with Chinese astrology and with numerology.

Come with me on this exploration of the "infinite variety" (in Shakespeare's phrase) of being a Gemini.

Joanna Martine Woolfolk
Stamford, Connecticut
June 2011

# GEMINI

## MAY 21–JUNE 20

# PART ONE

# ALL ABOUT YOU

# ILLUMINATING QUOTATIONS

"I succeeded by saying what everyone else is thinking."

—Joan Rivers, comedienne and author, a Gemini

"My music is best understood by children and animals."

—Igor Stravinsky, classical music composer, a Gemini

"If Galileo had said in verse that the world moved, the Inquisition might have let him alone."

—Thomas Hardy, novelist, a Gemini

"In school, I could hear the leaves rustle as they went off on a journey."

—Clint Eastwood, actor and director, a Gemini

"I wasn't really naked. I simply didn't have any clothes on."

—Josephine Baker, dancer, a Gemini

"If I'd observed all the rules, I'd never have gotten anywhere."

—Marilyn Monroe, actress, a Gemini

# YOUR GEMINI PERSONALITY

## YOUR MOST LIKEABLE TRAIT: Responsiveness

......................................................................................................

*The bright side of Gemini:* Witty, charming, amusing, winning
   social touch, quick-thinking, intelligent
*The dark side of Gemini:* Disorganized, inconsistent, superficial,
   cunning, manipulative

*You are lively, energetic, versatile, and intellectual. Your sign of
Gemini represents communication and the exchange of ideas. Curious and inquisitive, you want to learn and discover—and because
you fear missing out on anything, you want to be everywhere. As an
Air sign, you live primarily in your mind, entertaining possibilities
and seeing things from many perspectives. You're also a Mutable
sign, which means you're extremely adaptable to new situations.
Certainly you seek out new people, and your charm and spontaneity opens them to you. But being such a mental person, you tend to
divorce yourself from your emotions. Among other problems this
engenders, it keeps your relationships on a superficial level. You
seek personal freedom, and a strong streak of restlessness and dissatisfaction runs through your personality. You have trouble with
commitment and follow-through.*

The first thing people notice about you is the crackle of energy you give off. You're the one for whom the word *mercurial* was coined— the fastest thinker in the zodiac. Ruled by Mercury, winged messenger of the gods, yours is the sign of communication.

If all the world's a stage, you must be the actor on that stage. Unlike Leo, who wants only to be the star, Gemini wants to play *all* the parts—and be the director, the producer, and the stagehand!

Astrology regards Gemini as the most quintessentially human sign. It sums up qualities that are the distinguishing hallmarks of the human race—*intelligence* (you're an Air sign), *adaptability* (you're a Mutable sign), and *communicativeness* (ruled by Mercury).

As long as there's breath left in your body, you're going to use it to say something. You enjoy talking on the phone; tossing off e-mails, IMs, and text messages; and chatting with strangers. Born with the gift of persuasion, you could sell ice in Greenland. You've got more than a touch of Irish blarney—you've got pizzazz.

You're endlessly curious about everything. Your astrological symbol should really be the question mark. You're a perpetual student who never stops asking questions. A mental magpie, you pick up information here, gossip there, tidbits everywhere. This makes you an ideal conversationalist, for you know a little bit about everything—though, some have said, not a lot about anything. You're also inclined to have firm opinions on everything (subject to revision at a moment's notice). Your quick mind can explain any action, defend any position, justify any course.

What you value most is intellectual independence, and what you lack most is perseverance. Routine and monotony are two things you dread, and you will go to any length to avoid them. You want to be Alice in Wonderland racing from adventure to adventure. You love to explore new territory, to see the way people live on the other side of the world. You're open to a different way of looking at things.

It's the untried and original that keeps you interested. You constantly need new outlets, and your approach to anything novel is to try it at least once. "Who knows," you say, "maybe it's something I'll love forever. But I'll never know that unless I try it!"

Inquisitive and imaginative, for you the fun is in traveling, not in arriving at a destination. Your trendy, up-to-date lifestyle has you constantly living off the fad of the land. *Change* is your keyword because basically your nature is restless. A vein of discontent runs through you, a feeling of "is this all there is?"

Yet your facile gifts of writing, speaking, and self-expression do bring you much success. You have great skill dealing with the public, for your quicksilver personality can adapt to many kinds of people. Also, your amazing versatility enables you to jump into almost any situation. You're famous for the multiplicity of your talents. You write, compose, sing, act, dance. You're able to deal with personalities *and* with facts and figures.

At work, you're an innovator and planner, an outstanding performer in the most beguiling manner. Your charming way with people and special capacity for forming close working relationships contribute to your success. Plus you have a wide range of contacts, and benefit from the advice and help of influential people. You will definitely attract financial luck, though a tendency toward extravagance often more than offsets it. In your ledger, income always adds up to something a little short of outgo.

A pronounced trait of yours is *duality*—you need more than one creative pursuit, job, hobby, lover, and so forth. You're the kind of person who'll have two careers; juggle home, marriage, family, creative work, and social life; and still tell yourself, "If I could only get organized, I'd get so much *more* done!"

One reason you feel there's always more to get done is you tend to take on too much. As a result, you often leave a trail of unfinished tasks. You fritter away energy on too many projects instead of concentrating your cleverness on one task. Because you lose interest quickly, too often you're unable to demonstrate the depth of your extraordinary talent. Think how accomplished you'd be if you would stick to one thing long enough.

You also have difficulty with time management. You think five minutes have gone by when it really has been forty-five minutes. You're known for being late. Inwardly, you're high-strung and on your bad days irritable. You can become an overwrought thinker. Like a rat in a maze, you fret and worry and agonize over decisions. You cause yourself needless stress because in the end the right answer becomes apparent.

Another Gemini weakness is superficiality. Because you're so quick to grasp an idea or size up a situation, you tend to skim its surface, not bothering to explore it in depth. The other side of the coin is that with very little preparation you can make a marvelous initial impression.

You are often drawn to the stage and the dramatic arts. Some famous performers and writers born with the Sun in Gemini are Angelina Jolie, Marilyn Monroe, Ian Fleming, Clint Eastwood, Ken Follet, Morgan Freeman, and Joan Rivers.

Among the best things about you is the fact you're a wonderful friend who lifts people out of their doldrums. Does someone need advice? Instruction? An introduction? You're right there, ready to jump in, and others are energized by your enthusiasm. It's easy to see why you are usually surrounded by friends and admirers because you're such fun to be with. True, you can be a bit arrogant with persons who aren't as quick as you are or can't keep up with the rapid flow of your thought and speech. Still, your natural exuberance sweeps even the most reluctant and surly along with you. In almost any situation you can be as charming as you want to be—with a little extra thrown in.

However, you're uncomfortable plumbing dark emotional depths, and you certainly don't want to get sucked into anyone's problems that will sabotage your freedom. On the deepest level, you can be chillingly detached when you choose to be. If you no longer want to "hear" a person, you simply cancel out that person. You always begin a friendship thinking it will be forever, but should it run into serious conflict, you have a tendency to kill it and move on. Your method of punishment is to cut off communication. (There may be important people in your life to whom you purposely have not spoken for years.)

The other side of your twin personality is that you can be wonderfully generous with your advice, time, help, and interest. You have a special talent for involvement, a willingness to share. You believe most experiences are more rewarding if done in the company of others. Though you can become impatient with stodgy stick-in-the-muds, you have patience and generosity when it comes to helping someone in a jam.

For the most part, you hide the brooding side to your Jekyll and Hyde disposition. No one is better than you at beaming out good cheer and high spirits, and creating an atmosphere of fun and games. You bring sparkle and iridescence to others. For the sheer fascination of it, people should have at least one Gemini in their lives. (Two might be exhausting.)

# THE INNER YOU

You react instantly to new situations, but because you're so keenly attuned to your environment, you tend to have a nervous temperament. And though you give off sparks of energy, excitement, and charm, inside you feel like a wound-up spring. Others are fascinated by your enthusiasm while inwardly you're already bored with this person or that project. In your relationships, you're very giving, but you also need time for yourself. You like to perform, using your wit and intelligence to move to center stage. You love to gossip, mostly because you find out such interesting things! You're generous with your time, friendship, and possessions. One problem is that instead of looking at people's deeper qualities, you tend to judge them by their reaction to you. Are you coming off well; are you *mesmerizing* them? You're terribly caught up in having to be thought of as extraordinary.

# HOW OTHERS SEE YOU

People like to be around you because you're interesting and amusing. They admire you for your talent with words and sense of humor. They're drawn to you because you seem interested in them and ask them questions. Though you're considered more of a cerebral type, friends trust your judgment about emotional matters. They also know you'll jump in to help when asked. Only those closest to you know you can be moody and discouraged. When crossed you can be sarcastic, which makes some people think you're arrogant.

# GUARD AGAINST: Spreading Yourself Too Thin

Among your best qualities are flexibility and fluidity, for you're able to *adjust* (many cannot do this). And with your versatile skills, you can handle all kinds of fascinating projects. Your interest is piqued by an invitation, a possibility, and off you go.

But you try to go in all directions at once. Your tendency is to say yes to everything, and then you're overwhelmed by tasks hanging over you. Not least among many reasons for saying yes is you don't want to disappoint people who need you. Your instinct is to become involved and help solve problems. You feel you know what's needed and besides, this won't take long. You're famous for overestimating how much time and energy a job will take. There you are with a long to-do list; you give some of your tasks a lick and a promise while others wait. Nothing gets finished, much less well finished. As a Gemini, you're an idea person, but like the silken threads of a web, ideas can trap you. You don't practice the patient, hands-on, day-by-day focus on one goal until it's met.

You won't be able to concentrate on one thing until you channel your restlessness. You're like a wound-up clock (sometimes your nervous energy will erupt in physical conditions such as skin rashes and allergies). One of Gemini's profound lessons is to discover what great freedom there is in commitment.

The marvelous thing is, because of your curiosity and penetrating intelligence, you can become a great Renaissance person—someone who excels in a number of fields. This takes discipline (the *commitment* thing). You need to carefully choose those areas, keep the number of them limited, and not let yourself be tempted again and again by "one more" fascinating venture. Allow your strong Gemini mind to rule your decisions.

## YOUR GREATEST CHALLENGE:
### Learning to Listen to Your Heart

Gemini is the sign of intellectual sophistication but emotional ambivalence. With your brilliant reasoning powers, you think and ponder, rationalize and explain away. In your work, you're a smart puzzle and problem solver; you're able to provide answers and solutions. But the messy arena of relationships and convoluted feelings creates anxiety. You don't want to go near emotional depth. Instead, you go into the intellectual realm—you go into your head. You suppress and disconnect from emotions, lose your compassion, detach. In its darkest form, your cutting-off ability has a ruthlessness to it. When you're disconnected from your heart, you won't look at the chaos you create.

Yet you *are* Gemini—and within you exists the duality of head and heart, light and dark. You have the capacity to be whole. On some level you're aware of a certain hunger you need to fill; you're aware you crave more emotional richness in your life. By being courageous enough to feel uncomfortable feelings (anger, sadness, vulnerability), you will not only spare yourself the even deeper pain of emotional starvation, but find true completion.

Banal as it may sound to you, Gemini, *love* is the answer. Love yourself enough to honor your feelings, however conflicted they may be. Love others enough to be patient about the demands of being in a relationship with them. Love your work enough to focus on making it the best it can be. Like the Tin Man in *The Wizard of Oz*, you'll discover what a big heart you've always had!

## YOUR ALTER EGO

Astrology gives us many tools in our lives to help manage our struggles and solve problems. One of these tools is to reach into your opposite sign in the zodiac—your polarity. For you, Gemini, this is Sagittarius, sign of expansion and far vision. Astrologically, Gemini and Sagittarius are opposites with far more in common than any other pair of polarities. Sagittarius represents the quest for adventure and freedom, which certainly resonates with you, Gemini. Both signs are fascinated with knowledge and discovery, and both approach life with zest and optimism.

The basic difference is Gemini focuses on the *immediate*. You throw yourself into the busy passing scene and interact closely with people who stimulate you. You want to find out, explore, experiment, and stay *au courant*. Activity quickens your mind, which (like a computer) constantly needs information to keep humming along. You're all about picking up the pace. The result is that you can spin yourself into a psychically draining tizzy of overscheduling, overpromising, and trying over-hard to impress. You're high-strung to begin with, and to have unceasing demands on you makes you completely frazzled. You become angry and depressed that the world puts so much pressure on you.

Sagittarius, on the other hand, consciously flees from unworthy claims on its time and energy. Sagittarius's sights are on something greater—a plan of unusual proportion or a goal that embodies an idealistic vision. Sagittarius refuses to be limited to the narrow confines of other people's expectations or to get caught up in the petty (quarreling, gossiping). Its focus is to explore a wider world, to do something meaningful and magnificent that it hopes will benefit humanity. Sagittarius tends to think in terms of tomorrow—and this helps it to stay above the fray and on the important goal.

Gemini, the most important quality you can take from Sagittarius is to live your own truth (which is what Sagittarius does best). The nobility of the Sagittarian spirit centers on its honesty. If you, Gemini, can find your authentic voice and tap into who you truly are, you will free yourself from deep internal stress. Even if you just detach a little from what others think, you'll be able to stop living for their approval. And if you slow down and concentrate on what's important to *you*, you can turn a long-term aspiration into a reality.

In turn, Sagittarius has much to gain from its polarity—you, Gemini. Among the most valuable is your power with people, which has nothing to do with reliance on their good favor. You are resourceful, persuasive, and charismatic, and in the present moment. Sagittarius tends to be much more lost in big-time plans and far-fetched schemes. Sagittarius doesn't have your penchant for gathering facts and being up on the latest information. It could certainly use some of your social skills. Sagittarius would feel much more supported by a circle of friends if it cultivated contacts the way you do. With a bit of practical Gemini know-how, Sagittarius could unblock much of its creative output.

High on the list of what Sagittarius can glean from you is the power to be in the moment, the power of now. The present is all one really *has*—the past is over and the future isn't here yet. Sagittarius's tendency to live in a future not here yet robs Sagittarius of being alive right now!

# GEMINI IN LOVE

You're the world's best date—quick-witted, charming, generous, imaginative about places to go and things to see, and (most enticing of all) interested in your companion. Indeed, the secret to your allure is you're genuinely interested in people—what they have to say, how their minds work, what you can learn from them. In turn, prospective partners are drawn to your imagination and zest for living. You have a mesmerizing unpredictability.

Your love affairs, however, have a touch of the casual, and even when you become deeply involved or marry there's as much friendly feeling as heavy-breathing passion. Indeed, one of your favorite periods in a relationship is the intoxicating time when friendship is turning into love. For you, friendship and intellectual compatibility are primary—and without this kind of melding, even if you fall headlong into a brief sexual obsession, you just as quickly become bored. Gemini is a mental sign—your *mind* must be engaged.

Sometimes in the game of seduction you can appear heartless because, while trying to make the other person feel hopelessly enamored of you, you're also calculating whether that person is worthy of your attention. Furthermore, you're often not satisfied with just one lover on your string. You have a well-deserved reputation for being fickle and flirtatious.

This is because your dualistic nature demands more than one person can usually provide. To fulfill your needs, a lover must satisfy you on several planes at once: mental, emotional, *and* sexual. Therefore, the one with whom you fall deeply in love must truly be a composite person who can fill all your needs.

Many who are fascinated by you also think you're too difficult to figure out. But if they would keep your dual nature firmly in mind, they wouldn't be so confused. The deepest part of you is an intense romantic who keeps searching for true love. You were born under the sign of the Twins, and you're looking for your astral twin, your spiritual soulmate who will complete your nature and understand your complex personality.

Yet the other part of you needs stimulation and novelty. You may fantasize about being swept away by love, but in real life you're turned off by those who can't keep up with you. Many of the dates you go out on are a bust because the other person is just too dull. You don't have the patience, much less the *time*. And even though you have a connoisseur's appreciation for a really interesting lover, if an affair loses zest you look for the escape hatch. You need your minimum daily requirement of fun, and when the fun leaves so do you.

As a lover, you're passionate and generous, and you bring vivacious freshness to your lovemaking. You have an endless sexual curiosity and a charming willingness to experiment. You think sex is fascinating because it continually renews itself—it's the love part that so often becomes terminal. A common complaint from those involved with a Gemini is that Gemini fails on the emotional follow-through. You may be famous for being communicative, yet, oddly, you don't reveal yourself too openly or commit yourself too deeply.

Still, you tend to get involved with intense, emotional people. (Of course, you don't always *stay* involved.) Something about those who live on a dramatic level, who really feel emotions and express them, intrigues you. It's as though, through them, you hope to uncover a new facet in yourself.

Unconsciously, too, Gemini will play games in love, mainly mental games. You may work up a list of all the shortcomings of a partner, which you then subtly communicate. Should the person feel criticized and walk away, you decide how much more attractive he or she is than you originally thought.

A major problem is finding a lover with the perfect combination of intelligence, passion, strength, sensitivity, and a sense of adventure. Ultimately, when you do find this person, you'll move mountains to make him or her feel special. You share all of yourself. Underneath your bewildering variety of masks is a solid, enduring person, and your devotion is real. You're lavish with your affection and attention, and willing to help, advise, amuse, and encourage a lover in any way that's needed. Love, in fact, may bring out a latent jealous streak in you.

To the one who can offer both love and adventure, you are the world's best mate—a loyal, devoted lover and an endlessly fascinating companion.

# TIPS FOR THOSE WHO WANT TO ATTRACT GEMINI

Meet Gemini on high ground. Gemini's interests are wide rather than deep—they know a little about everything, but not much about any one thing. If you know one thing well, you'll impress them.

Gemini likes to give a friend or a lover a kind of IQ test. If you pass, you're welcome. You can even choose the subject on which you're being tested. Books, music, art, politics—Gemini is interested in all.

Beware of being too strongly conservative or conformist. In Gemini's scoring, this rates as dull. However, speak your mind frankly on any subject. Gemini admires candor and honesty, and a good exchange, even of contrary opinions, can be a firm foundation for better acquaintance.

Don't try to match wits, unless you're sure you have the verbal ammunition. Geminis of either gender wield words as weapons. Geminis enjoy intellectual talk, but they also love gossip. If you know any interesting anecdotes about the famous, the near-famous, or just mutual acquaintances, you'll have an appreciative audience. Geminis are also fond of anyone who can make them laugh.

Want to give a gift? Bracelets and rings will set off their expressive hands. Or give something that will stimulate Gemini's busy mind: books (or e-books), word games, puzzles, or interesting software; a laptop or the latest cell phone, Blackberry, or iPod; a CD that teaches a new language or a DVD of dance lessons.

Warning: Geminis are deeply sensitive, and they need to have people around whom they trust. Never give them a reason to suspect you are playing fast and loose with them (even if you are).

And don't you be suspicious of them; nothing distresses Geminis more than to have their motives distrusted.

## GEMINI'S EROGENOUS ZONES:
### Tips for Those with a Gemini Lover

Our bodies are very sensitive to the touch of another human being. The special language of touching is understood on a level more basic than speech. Each sign is linked to certain zones and areas of the body that are especially receptive and can receive sexual messages through touch. Many books and manuals have been written about lovemaking, but few pay attention to the unique knowledge of erogenous zones supplied by astrology. You can use astrology to become a better, more sensitive lover.

For Gemini, the hands and arms are especially receptive to erotic stimuli. Light kisses on this area, and brushes and fingertip touches, will send shivers of delight down a Gemini's spine. Gemini women are fond of hand kissers. Gemini men respond to light stroking of their hands, especially the palms and insides of the fingers. As a prelude to lovemaking, try lightly kissing the inside of your Gemini's arms, starting with his or her fingertips and moving up to the armpits.

A massage technique that natives of this sign find especially stimulating is to grip Gemini's wrist gently with both hands. Using light but firm pressure, turn one hand in one direction and the other in the opposite direction, in a gentle wringing motion. Do this all the way up Gemini's arm and down again. Another way to relax Gemini is to travel the path of his or her inner arm from the palm to the armpit, vibrating the flesh and muscles by using a circular motion on the skin with your fingertips.

# GEMINI'S AMOROUS COMBINATIONS: YOUR LOVE PARTNERS

## GEMINI AND ARIES

You're a lively, energetic pair who can be good friends as well as good lovers. Gemini and Aries both thrive on activity, adventure, and variety. You enjoy each other's humor and like social life. Each wants a partner who can keep up, and this you both do wonderfully. Adding to the effervescence are the bedroom high jinks, for you're both enthusiastic about sex. In the relationship, Aries will probably be the one to make the decisions because you have difficulty in that area. Aries can give you the firm direction you need, though a source of irritation is Aries's domineering streak. You dislike taking orders, and Aries will have to learn to soften its "my way or the highway" attitude. In general, Aries tends to be more focused on *its* needs than on yours, but Gemini's occasional wanderings from the straight and narrow will keep Aries on its toes.

## GEMINI AND TAURUS

An unpromising match, though at the beginning Taurus responds to the sparkle and joy you generate. You're intrigued by Taurus because of its romantic streak combined with an uncomplicated directness. Taurus is also steady and steadfast—but therein lies a major problem. Your focuses are too different. Taurus wants life to be stable and ordered, while you're easily bored and look for new experiences. Taurus is devoted to home sweet home, while you follow the lure of the open road. Sexually, you're not in tune. You like your erotica to have novelty and find Taurus's lovemaking a bit on the dull side. Emotionally, you also resent the restrictive net Taurus tries to construct. In turn, jealous, possessive Taurus can't handle your flirtatious manner with others and occasional outside dalliances. Passions cool.

## GEMINI AND GEMINI

No one will find a more versatile, charming, or vivacious pair than you. As Geminis, you both have the same strengths—openness to life and a gift for creating excitement. You'll never bore each other, for you're interested in everything. The pace is frenetic, but neither of you would dream of slowing down. You're fascinating conversationalists, have tons of friends, and together you'll throw some marvelous parties. Sex is fun and games, full of fantasy, and it's where you two communicate on a more complex level than you do with words. But Geminis also share the same weaknesses— impracticality, nervousness, irritability, and an inclination to evade responsibility. As a pair, you two are unstable and very restless.

When you move out of the bedroom, everything may become too chaotic—even for twin Geminis.

## GEMINI AND CANCER

Your irrepressible high spirits brighten Cancer's disposition, and passionate Cancer fulfills your physical needs. Cancer has a nurturing sexuality that makes you feel coddled and catered to. But all too soon, your Gemini tendency to play at love wounds oversensitive Cancer. You can't help being flirtatious, which makes Cancer feel very insecure. Your affair is likely to be volatile, filled with pent-up anger that erupts at unexpected moments. You have too little in common for a successful long-term relationship. Cancer needs security and domesticity; Gemini loathes being tied down. You have no patience with Cancer's moodiness, and the whiny, clingy hypersensitivity of Cancer drives you up a wall. Your sharp tongue is too biting for Cancer's fragile ego. As a partnership, you're doomed to a downhill run.

## GEMINI AND LEO

You two are an affectionate pair who really enjoy each other. Both of you have quick, inquisitive minds, and your affair usually starts off as a flirtatious friendship in which you try to match wits. You quickly become a hot item sexually. Gemini has amorous inventiveness and erotic fearlessness that find a responsive partner in eager, extroverted Leo. Leo's self-confidence blinks at the way you're always surrounded by lustful admirers, for Leo, too, is loaded with charisma. Of course, not everything in paradise is perfect. Your penchant for ridicule can annoy regal Leo, and Leo will probably demand more adoration than you're generally willing to give. Socially, each of you tries to upstage the other, but you have a lot of fun together doing it. You both love to laugh, and in bed you set off celestial sparklers. What more can you ask?

## GEMINI AND VIRGO

When you first meet, you two give off an intellectual energy that immediately connects you. You're intrigued by Virgo's knowledge, and Virgo is charmed by your inquisitiveness. The signs of Gemini and Virgo are both Mercury ruled and have a mental approach to life. But similarity ends there. You want to see bright possibilities, while Virgo sees everything that's wrong. Your relationship is star-crossed from the beginning. Virgo considers you scatterbrained and immature. You think of Virgo as a stick-in-the-mud and a bore. Virgo's analytical approach seems like indifference to you. Virgo looks on your busy social life as superficial and a waste of time. Virgo is critical; Gemini is tactless. Passions run on a low thermostat; your sex life soon turns chilly. Gemini's eye is certain to rove.

## GEMINI AND LIBRA

You two are Air signs who are well suited intellectually and in every other way. You quickly discover you're stimulating companions who in no time fall into a lovely affair. Neither is combative or controlling (which you find refreshing after previous fraught relationships), and you're likely to agree on everything. You both are affectionate and fun-loving, and you like social life, entertaining, and travel. Sexually, both are fervent, neither is jealous, and Libra goes along with Gemini's taste for experiment. In fact, sexually, you'll surprise each other, for together you'll uncover the deeper eroticism each has been looking for. Only a couple of problems mar the perfection. One is you both love to spend money. The other is Libra craves a bit more emotional understanding than Gemini detachment supplies. Still, you have so much in common it's almost a perfect match.

## GEMINI AND SCORPIO

Scorpio possesses magnetism (Gemini senses mystery and secrets) and, as a curious Gemini, you can't resist finding out more. Certainly, it would seem that your Gemini super-imagination and Scorpio's super-dynamism would make a good combination. But you two are simply unable to get along together. The one thing you have going is combustion in the bedroom, where sex can be wild and woolly—yet too soon you find out that sex isn't everything. Scorpio is sensual, passionate, demanding, jealous, inflexible. Gemini is lighthearted, nonchalant, changeable, and restless, pulled into myriad activities in which Scorpio is not the focus. You are a social creature; Scorpio likes privacy. Scorpio's suspicious nature is in constant turmoil over your casual attitude about love. It won't be long before enough becomes too much.

# GEMINI AND SAGITTARIUS

You two are opposites in the zodiac with much in common, and are attracted to each other like magnets. You'll especially enjoy each other's minds, for you both have wide-ranging and varied interests. Sagittarius tends to be more intellectual and immersed in ideas. You are more social and look for new activity. Certainly you both need freedom, and you're both restless and argumentative. Soon Sagittarius will consider you a fly-by-night and dilettante, and you'll see Sagittarius as pretentious in its "noble" self-view. Each of you is likely to be disappointed sexually, since neither is especially demonstrative—and you, Gemini, are very quick to criticize. (You want the experimentation of sex, and need someone skilled in erotic play to turn you on.) This affair probably began impulsively and will end the same way.

# GEMINI AND CAPRICORN

The immediate draw is that each has a quality the other thinks it wants. You're taken with Capricorn's strength of purpose, and Capricorn responds to your sparkle and generous warmth. But in no time the stark differences in your styles, outlooks, and aspirations become all too apparent. Your freewheeling, anything-goes attitude meets opposition from conventional, steady, conservative Capricorn. Capricorn worries about security, while you fret about losing your liberty. Order and routine keep Capricorn content but drive a Gemini to distraction. Your need for a stimulating existence does nothing to make Capricorn feel secure. And Capricorn's sober outlook puts a damper on your Gemini high spirits. Nor is this an affair with high sexual voltage, although you can help develop Capricorn's sensual potential.

## GEMINI AND AQUARIUS

The two of you are Air signs who most of all need a communion of mind and spirit—and find this in each other. Versatile Gemini and innovative Aquarius get along famously. You share a taste for novelty, travel, and meeting new people. Aquarius is more the oddball and doesn't care what others think, whereas you focus on being charming. Aquarius is also more stubborn than you. You're both unpredictable, which lends an air of spontaneity although it also means things can't always go smoothly. Still, love keeps getting better, for Aquarius adores your wit and good cheer. You two enjoy a spicy sex life, and if you're somewhat inconstant or unstable, Aquarius understands. If the affair should end, you'll still remain friends. In marriage, you two are affectionate, devoted companions more than passionate lovers.

## GEMINI AND PISCES

The passion quotient is high, and so are the problems. Emotional Pisces is too easily hurt by your casual, careless ways and numerous outside interests. Your personality is mischievous and playful, but Pisces is sensitive and takes things to heart. You each practice deception in your own way: Gemini dissembles, Pisces won't deal with reality. What keeps you together far longer than it should is your intense sexual rapport. Pisces is a fantasy addict who'll go to any length to please, and Gemini is into sex with an innovative edge. Beyond this, you both crave different things. You need free-dom and new vistas; Pisces needs unending devotion. Pisces just can't feel secure with gadabout Gemini and tries to pull the net tighter. The claustrophobic atmosphere eventually makes it hard for you to breathe.

# YOUR GEMINI CAREER PATH

The reason Gemini has a hard time deciding what to do in life is you can do so many things well. Early on, you tend to bounce around looking for your passion (and taking criticism for not sticking to one thing). But this is good training for later, when you're handling many aspects of a given profession. Your wide-ranging knowledge is a key element in your success—as is your openness to new opportunity.

You're also blessed with intuitive brilliance. For example, you can attempt a task you know little about and have never done before and, in short order, outperform those with experience. Your best career assets are your originality and a winning way with people. You communicate well and have cheery enthusiasm. These Gemini attributes are particularly valuable when linked in partnership with someone more practical and hardheaded. For example, you'd make a great overseer of a project in which you designed, did research, were the spokesperson, and dealt with the public, but you'd need a sidekick or assistant to keep you from getting sidetracked.

In general, you're less interested in power than in doing something interesting with your life, something that gives you autonomy and stimulation. Rather than deal with VIPs in the boardroom, you'd like to interact with them at A-list parties. You enjoy networking with people because they can give you information or open a new subject. And you like to perform and show your style. Also, those high-powered careers tend to keep you in one spot—in the same office with the same people. Gemini needs to be out and about, freer.

Certainly, Gemini versatility sets you apart from the crowd. Others may plod along doing one chore at a time, but you keep many balls in the air. You're best suited for a career that allows you to use your skill with words. You make an excellent writer, journalist, lecturer, critic, commentator, and teacher. With your natural gregariousness, you'd be a wonderful talk-show host, and certainly, as a communicator, you were born to work in the media. Agenting is successful for you (e.g., in real estate, travel, or show business). The field of public relations is ripe with opportunity, as is the sales arena. You have a visually creative sense and can do jewelry or graphic design. You're a warm, congenial host and would do well owning a restaurant or bar.

Whatever field you choose, just make sure you're not desk-bound—you need plenty of space and movement. Also, the real secret to finding work that fulfills is to never let your active mind be bored. You must have stimulation; avoid day-to-day routine. You need a mix—people, travel, time alone—and always something in which your mind is creating.

Gemini is known as a Peter Pan, but the issues around this go deeper than just needing "freedom." One underlying reason for your difficulty committing to a course is lack of confidence (which few people see). An example of this is your reluctance to confront a superior about a raise or better working conditions, and instead opting to look for something else. When you can push past your fears (your performance anxiety, fear of not being seen as smart and dazzling, fear of conflict), the goals that are truly in your heart will become the most important thing. That is when you will commit to your true Gemini calling.

# GEMINI AND HEALTH: ADVICE FROM ASTROLOGY

*For optimum health, you need a combination of exercise, recreation, and relaxation. Gemini tends to be wound up like a too-tight spring, and you live with jangled nerves. You silently fret, worsening your nervous tension. With your mind in overdrive, you neglect your physical needs, and problems with insomnia only send you into a deeper stress spiral. Exercise is the antidote. It pumps up energy—which is completely different from frenetic activity. With healthy energy, you're far less perturbed and far more productive. Also, in its magic way, exercise calms and soothes and creates positive feelings, all of which counteracts a Gemini propensity toward depression. Monotony, too, can bring you down; definitely, friendships and social life, pleasant pastimes, and creative hobbies also divert you into pathways of well-being.*

Advice and useful tips about health are among the most important kinds of information that astrology provides. Health and well-being are of paramount concern to human beings. Love, money, or career takes second place, for without good health we cannot enjoy anything in life.

Astrology and medicine have had a long marriage. Hippocrates (born around 460 B.C.), the Greek philosopher and physician who is considered the father of medicine, said, "A physician without a knowledge of astrology has no right to call himself a physician." Indeed, up until the eighteenth century, the study of astrology and its relationship to the body was very much a part of a doctor's training. When a patient became ill, a chart was immediately drawn up. This guided the doctor in both diagnosis and treatment, for the chart would tell when the crisis would come and what medicine would help. Of course, modern Western doctors no longer use astrology to treat illness. However, astrology can still be a useful tool in helping to understand and maintain our physical well-being.

## THE PART OF THE BODY RULED BY GEMINI

Each sign of the zodiac governs a specific part of the body. These associations date back to the beginning of astrology. Curiously, the part of the body that a sign rules is in some ways the strongest and in other ways the weakest area for natives of that sign.

Your sign of Gemini rules the shoulders, arms, hands, and lungs. You're noted for your graceful arms and beautifully shaped hands. While speaking you tend to gesticulate with your hands. You're dexterous and well coordinated, and often excel at sports and dancing. You're known as a jack-of-all-trades who is happiest when involved with many projects and a wide range of people. As a Gemini, you're blessed in that you keep looking young far longer than others do.

You are, however, vulnerable to upper respiratory infections, bronchitis, and asthma. In times of stress you may have difficulty breathing and suffer from either hyperventilation or an inability to draw in enough oxygen. You're prone toward getting sprains and fractures, particularly in the bones of the shoulders, arms, or hands. You're also afflicted by bumps, cuts, scratches, and bruises.

Gemini rules the nerves, and thus you tend to be excitable and high-strung. You vacillate between despondency and euphoria, and seem to run on your nerves. The planet Mercury, which rules Gemini, has always been associated with respiration, the brain, and the entire nervous system. It also governs the delicate links between mind and the different parts of the body. An example of how nerves can affect you is that at times your inner stress exhibits itself in skin rashes, eruptions, and breakouts. You need to find ways to calm and "even out" your nerves. Your state of mind has a great deal to do with the state of your health—anxiety and nervousness literally can make you sick.

## DIET AND HEALTH TIPS FOR GEMINI

Relaxation is not just something nice if you can get it. It's essential to your well-being. Because you expend so much nervous energy, you need to take time to unwind, relax, and soothe your jangled nerves. Coffee and stimulants make matters worse and should be avoided. Herbal teas have a calming effect.

You're inclined to eat on the run—Geminis are notorious junk-food addicts. To keep up your energy and high spirits, you must have a proper diet. Many Geminis can't tolerate large amounts of food at one time; eating four minimeals a day can be beneficial.

The cell salt* for Gemini is potassium chloride, which builds fibrin (a fibrous protein) in the blood, organs, and tissues. A deficiency of this mineral leads to clots in the blood and circulatory problems. Potassium chloride also keeps the lungs and bronchial tubes unclogged. Foods high in this mineral are asparagus, green beans, tomatoes, celery, carrots, spinach, oranges, peaches, plums, apricots, and wild rice. Healthy nerve foods for Gemini include grapefruit, almonds, broiled fish and shellfish, grape juice, apples, and raisins. Lettuce and cauliflower help to combat bronchitis. You need calcium to keep your bones healthy; milk, buttermilk, and cottage cheese are excellent sources.

You should protect your chest in cold, inclement weather, and never smoke tobacco. Not only is smoking detrimental to the lungs, it causes circulatory problems in the arms and hands. Practice deep-breathing or yoga exercises to help you relax and breathe easier. Playing tennis and ping-pong will strengthen your arms.

*Cell salts (also known as tissue salts) are mineral compounds found in human tissue cells. These minerals are the only substances our cells cannot produce by themselves. The life of cells is relatively short, and the creation of new cells depends on the presence of these minerals.

# THE DECANATES AND CUSPS OF GEMINI

*Decanate* and *cusp* are astrological terms that subdivide your Sun sign. These subdivisions further define and emphasize certain qualities and character traits of your Sun sign, Gemini.

## WHAT IS A DECANATE?

Each astrological sign is divided into three parts, and each part is called a *decanate* or a *decan* (the terms are used interchangeably).

The word comes from the Greek word *dekanoi*, meaning "ten days apart." The Greeks took their word from the Egyptians, who divided their year into 360 days.* The Egyptian year had twelve months of thirty days each, and each month was further divided into three sections of ten days each. It was these ten-day sections that the Greeks called *dekanoi*.

*The Egyptians soon found out that a 360-day year was inaccurate, and so added on five extra days. These were feast days and holidays, and not counted as real days.

Astrology still divides the zodiac into decanates. There are twelve signs in the zodiac, and each sign is divided into three decanates. You might picture each decanate as a room. You were born in the sign of Gemini, which consists of three rooms (decanates). In which room of Gemini were you born?

The zodiac is a 360-degree circle. Each decanate is ten degrees of that circle, or about ten days long, since the Sun moves through the zodiac at approximately the rate of one degree per day. (This is not exact, because not all of our months contain thirty days.)

The decanate of a sign does not change the basic characteristics of that sign, but it does refine and individualize the sign's general characteristics. If you were born, say, in the second decanate of Gemini, it does not change the fact you are Gemini. It does indicate that you have somewhat special characteristics, different from those of Gemini people born in the first decanate or the third decanate.

Finally, each decanate has a specific planetary ruler, sometimes called a subruler because it does not usurp the overall rulership of your sign. The subruler can only enhance and add to the distinct characteristics of your decanate. For example, your entire sign of Gemini is ruled by Mercury, but the second decanate of Gemini is subruled by Venus. The influence of Venus, the subruler, combines with the overall authority of Mercury to make the second decanate of Gemini unlike any other in the zodiac.

## FIRST DECANATE OF GEMINI

May 21 through May 31
*Keyword*: Ingenuity

*Constellation*: Lepus, the Hare, who triumphs over enemies by outwitting them.
*Planetary subruler*: Mercury

Mercury is both your ruler and subruler, and your mental acumen is sharp. You enjoy new ideas and look for chances to express yourself. Your ability to speak or write influences the direction of your life. You have a forceful personality because you're able to decide quickly and then act. Logic and rationality are two rules you live by; you try not to cloud issues by sentimentalizing them. This is not to say you don't have warm feelings. You have a genuine capacity for forming close relationships, and if you love someone you tend to involve yourself completely in that person's affairs. You are nurturing and devoted. Underneath you are a tense worrier who suffers and frets too much. You try to handle all details brilliantly, but often they overwhelm you.

## SECOND DECANATE OF GEMINI

June 1 through June 10
*Keyword*: Union
*Constellation*: Orion, the Giant Hunter of magnificent strength and beauty. Orion was placed in the heavens to commemorate his great bravery.
*Planetary subruler*: Venus

Harmonious Venus combines with Gemini's Mercury to give you a deft social touch. People respond to your warm and effusive nature. The approval and esteem of others are important to you, and you tend to function best with people rather than as a loner.

There is a sense of adventure in your outlook, and you enjoy travel because it exposes you to new experiences. Once you have made up your mind about a pursuit, you eagerly give it your best effort. Sharing is part of your life, and you are generous with your time and friendship, and also with possessions. You have a great deal of sex appeal and are ardent in your expression of love. At times you can be argumentative because you are so fond of your own ideas.

## THIRD DECANATE OF GEMINI

June 11 through June 20
*Keyword*: Reason
*Constellation*: Auriga, the Charioteer. He was the serpent-footed king who invented the four-wheeled chariot, which symbolizes communication.
*Planetary subruler*: Uranus

Uranus, planet of knowledge, combines with Gemini's Mercury to give you clear and perceptive reasoning powers. You are known for your original point of view, and people often seek your advice. You have power to generate enthusiasm in others, a talent you'll utilize to further your aims. You tend to be intellectual, and approach life on a mental rather than an emotional basis. Though you have many friendships and love affairs, it's your mind that must be first engaged before your heart can follow. In your work, you take the practical approach and disregard anything you cannot put to use. You are both witty and loquacious, and never reluctant to say what you think. At times you are too demanding and domineering, for you expect others to live up to your high standards.

# WHAT IS A CUSP?

A *cusp* is the point at which a new astrological sign begins.* Thus, the cusp of Gemini means the point at which Gemini begins. (The word comes from the Latin word *cuspis*, meaning "point.")

When someone speaks of being "born on the cusp," that person is referring to a birth time at or near the beginning or the end of an astrological sign. For example, if you were born on June 20, you were born on the cusp of Cancer, the sign that begins on June 21. Indeed, depending on what year you were born, your birth time might even be in the first degree of Cancer. People born on the very day a sign begins or ends are often confused about what sign they really are—a confusion made more complicated by the fact that the Sun does not move into or out of a sign at *exactly* the same moment (or even day) each year. There are slight time differences from year to year. Therefore, if you are a Gemini born on May 21 or June 20, you'll find great clarity consulting a computer chart that tells you exactly where the Sun was at the very moment you were born.

As for what span of time constitutes being born on the cusp, the astrological community holds various opinions. Some astrologers claim *cusp* means being born only within the first two days or last two days of a sign (though many say this is too narrow a time frame). Others say it can be as much as within the first ten days or last ten days of a sign (which many say is too wide an interpretation). The consensus is that you were born on the cusp if your birthday is within the first *five* days or last *five* days of a sign.

The question hanging over cusp-born people is, "What sign am I really?" They feel they straddle the border of two different

---

*In a birth chart, a cusp is also the point at which an astrological House begins.

countries. To some extent, this is true. If you were born on the cusp, you're under the influence of both signs. However, much like being a traveler leaving one country and crossing into another, you must actually *be* in one country—you can't be in two countries at the same time. One sign is always a stronger influence, and that sign is almost invariably the sign that the Sun was actually in (in other words, your Sun sign). The reason I say "almost" is that in rare cases a chart may be so heavily weighted with planets in a certain sign that the person more keenly feels the influence of that specific sign.

For example, I have a client who was born in the evening on June 20. On that evening, the Sun was leaving Gemini and entering Cancer. At the moment of her birth the Sun was still in Gemini, so technically speaking she is a Gemini. However, the Sun was only a couple hours away from being in Cancer, and this person has the Moon, Mercury, and Venus all in Cancer. She has always felt like a Cancer and always behaved as a Cancer.

This, obviously, is an unusual case. Generally, the Sun is the most powerful planetary influence in a chart. Even if you were born with the Sun on the very tip of the first or last degree of Gemini, Gemini is your Sun sign—and this is the sign you will most feel like.

Still, the influence of the approaching sign or of the sign just ending is present, and you will probably sense that mixture in yourself.

......................................................................................................

# BORN MAY 21 THROUGH MAY 25

......................................................................................................

You are Gemini with Taurus tendencies. You are inquisitive and changeable, but you also have a stubborn streak and are not easily moved off your course. At times you become irritable when others don't measure up to your expectations. Generally, though, you deal tactfully with others, and you have many friends. You have a pronounced romantic streak. Artistic or musical talent may be evident, but you are practical and realistic about making money. Your attitude in new situations is, "Where do *I* fit in?" Usually you make a marvelous first impression.

## BORN JUNE 16 THROUGH JUNE 20

You are Gemini with Cancer tendencies. You are quick-witted and communicative, and also analytical, cautious, and conservative in your approach. When you give your word, others know they can trust you to do exactly as you say. You like to be surrounded with familiar objects and people, and you put a lot of weight on charming manners and appearance. Yours is a sensitive nature that loves deeply and is easily hurt by carelessness or selfishness. You are not satisfied with being ordinary; you want to create beauty or be known for your brilliance.

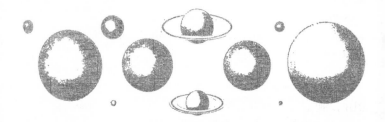

# YOUR SPECIAL DAY OF BIRTH

......................................................................

## MAY 21

......................................................................

You are goal oriented, and, unlike many Geminis, you have fierce stick-to-it-iveness. You also have great social charm and a persuasive way with people. In love, you give of yourself intensely.

......................................................................

## MAY 22

......................................................................

Your ability to "know" things in a flash sets you apart—you get the picture immediately. Whether or not you choose to, you always find yourself directing others. In love, your heart is easily broken.

......................................................................

## MAY 23

......................................................................

You are loved for your cheery generosity. Routine would be good for you, but your life constantly flies outward and becomes chaotic. Romantically, you need a partner who provides ballast.

## MAY 24

You personify versatility and make everything you touch look easy. People don't see the nervous intensity underneath. You tend to be shy at the beginning of a love relationship, but a lover quickly finds how sexual you are.

## MAY 25

You have a soft heart and wild sense of humor—but also a sharp eye for facts and figures and seeing deeply into other people's motives. Finding perfect love may be a long journey, for you search for grand passion.

## MAY 26

You're restless and live frenetically. But you also have a heart that nourishes, and your real success comes out of relationships. People are devoted to you. Because of your sex appeal, love can get complicated.

## MAY 27

Because you're so easygoing, people think they can change you. But you have stubbornness and will do only what *you* value. You have a committed heart—in time you'll find the work and the lover that stay forever.

# MAY 28

You're charismatic *and* adaptable—a blend of personal magnetism and "people smarts." It's only your difficulty in making decisions that can stand in the way of success. Love brings out a hidden possessive streak.

# MAY 29

You are a force of nature—outspoken and very definite in your views. You have grand plans, and what you undertake you give yourself to. It takes a special lover to understand your hungry heart.

# MAY 30

You are intellectually gifted and have a strong sense of duty. You're able to take responsibility and will go far. Yet along with your mental approach, you have emotional passion. You love with abandon.

# MAY 31

You have a hardworking side, but the other part is fun loving and seeks pleasure and exotic experiences. You're expressive; communication is your strong point in your career. You may have a number of lovers before you commit.

## JUNE 1

You're ambitious, have a sense of purpose, and display great taste. People trust your opinions. Beneath your practical exterior you have a secret recklessness, especially in love. You believe in fate.

## JUNE 2

Your abundant talent makes people see you as formidable. Yet you're warm, giving, enticing, and approachable. Your quick mind works well in crisis mode. Love can be confusing because you're so vulnerable.

## JUNE 3

Luck and love are your guardian angels, though you must find your way through a dark forest before you realize you're protected. You're destined for creative success and (at last) a lover who puts you first.

## JUNE 4

Your persona may be flighty and ethereal, but underneath you're solid and steadfast. You have a clever and resourceful mind for business. When you're in love, you display a great deal of romantic/ sexual energy.

## JUNE 5

You were born with basic self-esteem you can always draw on. You think deeply about things, and your insight into people makes it seem you can read minds. In love, you allow the real you to be seen only when you trust.

## JUNE 6

You're a true Twin. You are bubbly and outgoing, with a life filled with admirers. But your dark side emerges at odd moments, and you must fight off demons. In love, you need a lot of physical and emotional attention.

## JUNE 7

Your heart is filled with great expectations, and these will surely unfold. You have an extraordinary talent that you need to focus on. You can change people's lives. Your love lesson is that you will receive what you give.

## JUNE 8

You have an easy, balanced demeanor that belies a detective's probing mind. You can do unusual and original work and also deal gracefully with people. Love is often a performance until someone special rips away the veil.

## JUNE 9

You have an appetite for life, and early on learned how strong you are. You'll do work that's different from others'. You're also loving and passionate, but through experience have come to see not every lover can be trusted.

## JUNE 10

People are drawn to your perceptive mind and your inclusive way of accepting them. You were born at a special time—luck will always bail you out. Believe in true love; you're one of the rare ones who will find it.

## JUNE 11

Stay on a creative path, for you're blessed with talent. You have a way of attracting people with complicated emotional baggage. Life is a soap opera, but you're promised passion and a happy ending to a love story.

## JUNE 12

You're a fast thinker and communicator nonpareil—but your big heart is the success factor in your work and relationships. The only fly in the ointment is your tendency in love to sacrifice and put yourself last.

## JUNE 13

You have a talk-show host personality wrapped in a glamorous, theatrical appearance. You have deep wells of generosity, but you can also be exacting and imperious. Happiness in love may be elusive until you truly follow your heart.

## JUNE 14

You're an instigator of change, which is good, for you're skilled and uncommonly intelligent. Your aspirations will come true. In love, you have high standards, and then you're suddenly swept away.

## JUNE 15

You were born to perform and make an impact on the public. Your talent can create an amazing body of work. Your lesson is to learn self-sufficiency. In love, you're a rescuer, but you also have a strong survival instinct.

## JUNE 16

You're unorthodox and a revolutionary, but you cloak this with the sweetest manner with people. In work, you're a "closer" (you get to your target)—and in love, you're a runaway romantic with an off-putting outer shell.

## JUNE 17

You're a fast-track person constantly hurtling forward, yet also deeply traditionalist. You are caring and nurturing, and you honor the past. You have a passionate heart, and when you find true love you are devotedly faithful.

## JUNE 18

You have a commanding presence and an expansive intelligence. You're a gifted writer, a lover of the arts, blessed with style that others emulate. Love relationships will be turbulent until you find your own calm center.

## JUNE 19

You're an artist in business, and in creative work you possess a skill for making money. You have inner courage you must discover for yourself. Romantically, you're in love with love and need someone to tap into your fantasy.

## JUNE 20

You're like a visitor from another planet—in this world but not exactly *of* it. When you accept how different you are and use those differences, love, happiness, successful work, and financial reward all open.

# YOU AND CHINESE ASTROLOGY

With Marco Polo's adventurous travels in A.D. 1275, Europeans learned for the first time of the great beauty, wealth, history, and romance of China. Untouched as they were by outside influences, the Chinese developed their astrology along different lines from other ancient cultures, such as the Egyptians, Babylonians, and Greeks in whose traditions Western astrology has its roots. Therefore the Chinese zodiac differs from the zodiac of the West. To begin with, it's based on a lunar cycle rather than Western astrology's solar cycle. The Chinese zodiac is divided into twelve years, and each year is represented by a different animal—the rat, ox, tiger, rabbit, dragon, snake, horse, goat, monkey, rooster, dog, or pig. The legend of the twelve animals is that when Buddha lay on his deathbed, he asked the animals of the forest to come and bid him farewell. These twelve were the first to arrive. The cat, as the story goes, is not among the animals because it was napping and couldn't be bothered to make the journey. (In some Asian countries, however, such as Vietnam, the cat replaces the rabbit.)

Like Western astrology, in which the zodiac signs have different characteristics, each of the twelve Chinese animal years assigns character traits specific to a person born in that year. For example, the Year of the Rat confers honesty and an analytical mind, whereas the Year of the Monkey grants charm and a quick ability to spot opportunity.

Here are descriptions for Gemini for each Chinese animal year:

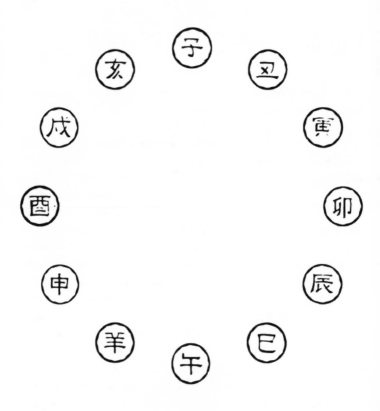

# IF YOU ARE GEMINI BORN IN THE YEAR OF THE RAT

## Years of the Rat

| | | | |
|---|---|---|---|
| 1900 | 1960 | 2020 | 2080 |
| 1912 | 1972 | 2032 | 2092 |
| 1924 | 1984 | 2044 | |
| 1936 | 1996 | 2056 | |
| 1948 | 2008 | 2068 | |

In Asian astrology, the Rat is full of charm and a cheery seductiveness. Rats are nimble socially and have a special people-charisma. These shining qualities blend beautifully with your Gemini ability to adapt and persuade and, in general, be a communicator extraordinaire. As a Gemini Rat, you have elegant creativity and a radiant spirit—you light up the humdrum and ordinary. You're also an audacious leader with ambitious ideas, although some would say you can be meddling and faultfinding. However, you're known for your kindness to strangers and your true devotion to family and friends. You give of yourself. Sexually, you're skilled at erotic technique and generous in pleasing a lover. Compatible partners are born in the Years of the Monkey, Pig, Rat, and Snake.

## Years of the Ox

| | | | |
|---|---|---|---|
| 1901 | 1961 | 2021 | 2081 |
| 1913 | 1973 | 2033 | 2093 |
| 1925 | 1985 | 2045 | |
| 1937 | 1997 | 2057 | |
| 1949 | 2009 | 2069 | |

The Year of the Ox personifies patience and equanimity, an ability to roll with the punches—and these qualities strengthen your eclectic intelligence as well as calm down your Gemini propensity for flitting off too soon. The combination of Gemini charisma and Ox determination makes you formidable when you set your heart on something. You work hard, get places, and have little use for slackers. The Ox also adds eloquence to your Gemini gift of gab. Your desire is for excellence. Gemini Ox has deep feelings and huge stores of sensitivity, which you tend to hide unless you know a person well. Love brings out your best and worst. You're intensely romantic and fall profoundly into passion, but you're also too possessive. Compatible partners are born in the Years of the Rabbit, Rooster, Monkey, Pig, and Snake.

# IF YOU ARE GEMINI BORN IN THE YEAR OF THE TIGER

## Years of the Tiger

| | | | |
|---|---|---|---|
| 1902 | 1962 | 2022 | 2082 |
| 1914 | 1974 | 2034 | 2094 |
| 1926 | 1986 | 2046 | |
| 1938 | 1998 | 2058 | |
| 1950 | 2010 | 2070 | |

The Tiger is aristocratic, swift, and beautiful, and to Buddhists a symbol of spiritual evolvement. As a Gemini Tiger you have personal dazzle—a combination of style and a way of engendering affectionate feelings in others. With your superquick mind and chemistry with a crowd, you can't help seizing the attention of an audience. You also have noble qualities of standing up for your principles, being a bold adventurer, and lighting the world with your optimistic outlook. For career happiness, you need to concentrate on your passion. Emotionally, your main difficulties center on intimacy; you have issues with trust and letting go of control. In bed, you're definitely a ferocious tiger. Compatible partners are born in the Years of the Rabbit, Dog, Dragon, Monkey, Pig, and Tiger.

## Years of the Rabbit

| | | | |
|---|---|---|---|
| 1903 | 1963 | 2023 | 2083 |
| 1915 | 1975 | 2035 | 2095 |
| 1927 | 1987 | 2047 | |
| 1939 | 1999 | 2059 | |
| 1951 | 2011 | 2071 | |

There's nothing timorous or timid about the Asian Rabbit. Rabbit people are talkative and theatrical, and they have rich imaginations—traits that blend seamlessly with your Gemini flash and magnetic likability. As a Gemini Rabbit, you draw from an endless wellspring of ideas, plans, observations, and useful information. You're good at business and at working with quarrelsome people, for you have charm. Rabbits are *fertile*, which applies to your mind, creativity, body, and sexuality. Unfortunately, your Gemini tendency to be distracted and overscheduled is doubly accented. In love, you need someone who can calm your nervous temperament, yet keep up with your fast pace. Sexually, you search for new ways to keep the fantasy level high. Compatible partners are born in the Years of the Goat, Dog, Dragon, Snake, Horse, and Monkey.

# IF YOU ARE GEMINI BORN IN THE YEAR OF THE DRAGON

### Years of the Dragon

| | | | |
|---|---|---|---|
| 1904 | 1964 | 2024 | 2084 |
| 1916 | 1976 | 2036 | 2096 |
| 1928 | 1988 | 2048 | |
| 1940 | 2000 | 2060 | |
| 1952 | 2012 | 2072 | |

The imperial Dragon signifies *magnitude* in every sense—and Dragon people are said to be abundantly generous and have superstar personalities. Add this to your Gemini dash and expressiveness, and the result is someone others characterize as unforgettable. You gravitate toward unusual work, have a way of dressing and behaving that sets you apart, and hold startling opinions. You may want to fit in with others but can't help being a "character." You're fierce in following your dreams and definitely believe in doing things your way. You don't like being crossed and are a stickler for the rules (your rules)—but people respond to your intense warmth. Love relationships are a dramatic rollercoaster ride, and sexually you're red-hot. Compatible partners are born in the Years of the Rabbit, Goat, Monkey, Snake, and Tiger.

### Years of the Snake

| | | | |
|---|---|---|---|
| 1905 | 1965 | 2025 | 2085 |
| 1917 | 1977 | 2037 | 2097 |
| 1929 | 1989 | 2049 | |
| 1941 | 2001 | 2061 | |
| 1953 | 2013 | 2073 | |

The sensuous Snake is associated with the Japanese love goddess, and throughout Asia symbolizes an ability to elicit adoration. The Year of the Snake confers superiority, and, as a Gemini Snake, you have a special grace. You make everything look easy. You may strive intensely (and often struggle), but your outer demeanor gives the message that you're born to succeed at everything you touch. Not only does your Gemini intelligence quickly grasp concepts, you can intuitively read people to your advantage. Money is an issue, for you're both extravagant and tightfisted, and others find it hard to know when each side will emerge. Love, sex, and creativity are your true passions—you're incurably romantic and also erotically driven. Compatible partners are born in the Years of the Rabbit, Rooster, Dragon, Horse, Ox, and Rat.

# IF YOU ARE GEMINI BORN IN THE YEAR OF THE HORSE

## Years of the Horse

| | | | |
|------|------|------|------|
| 1906 | 1966 | 2026 | 2086 |
| 1918 | 1978 | 2038 | 2098 |
| 1930 | 1990 | 2050 | |
| 1942 | 2002 | 2062 | |
| 1954 | 2014 | 2074 | |

The Year of the Horse carries extraordinary power. (In China, pregnancies are planned around Horse years.) Horse people embody the principle of power that's harnessed, which brings deeper dimension to your Gemini ability to sway the public. As a Gemini Horse, you're especially gregarious, assertive, and influential, as well as being intensely persuasive. Horse "wildness" adds to your Gemini creative fire. You have an instinct for the fantastic idea that can generate money. You don't have patience for those who dilly-dally. You make decisions with your gut, knowing you're right 99 percent of the time. You can be a hard taskmaster. In love, too, you want to control, but this rarely happens. You fall headlong into lust and are swept away. Compatible partners are born in the Years of the Rabbit, Rooster, Goat, Horse, and Snake.

# IF YOU ARE GEMINI BORN IN THE YEAR OF THE GOAT

(羊)

Years of the Goat

| | | | |
|---|---|---|---|
| 1907 | 1967 | 2027 | 2087 |
| 1919 | 1979 | 2039 | 2099 |
| 1931 | 1991 | 2051 | |
| 1943 | 2003 | 2063 | |
| 1955 | 2015 | 2075 | |

The Chinese teach that Goat people are able to carve out a life of adventure that also provides stability. The Goat is an amalgam of fey charm, artistic brilliance, and a lovable personality. These qualities merge with your Gemini intelligence and communicative power to make you a standout, professionally and socially. You have courage and honesty and the spirit of a winner. You also have emotional depth. You read, gather information, question things, and ponder the meaning beneath the apparent meaning. You're a more profound thinker than other Geminis. A streak of dissatisfaction runs through you, and at odd times you're lazy and undisciplined. You have an amorous, flirtatious nature and can be a sucker for the promise of erotic passion. Compatible partners are born in the Years of the Rabbit, Dragon, Horse, Monkey, and Pig.

# IF YOU ARE GEMINI BORN IN THE YEAR OF THE MONKEY

申

## Years of the Monkey

| | | | |
|---|---|---|---|
| 1908 | 1968 | 2028 | 2088 |
| 1920 | 1980 | 2040 | 2100 |
| 1932 | 1992 | 2052 | |
| 1944 | 2004 | 2064 | |
| 1956 | 2016 | 2076 | |

In the Asian zodiac, the Monkey is the beloved companion to the God of Travel—underlining the premise that Monkey people are vivacious, whimsical entertainers with irrepressible spirit. The Year of the Monkey bestows inventiveness, a gift for laughter, and loquacious charm—all of which sharpens your Gemini curiosity and gives you greater daring. As a Gemini Monkey, your destiny is to explore a field of expertise others wouldn't touch, and find fame as an orator, writer, and dispenser of knowledge. People think you're psychic because of your uncanny observations and ability to uncover others' secrets. You can be a devastating lover—you create illusion and weave a sexual spell, and your past is littered with liaisons. Compatible partners are born in the Years of the Rabbit, Dragon, Ox, Pig, Rat, and Tiger.

# IF YOU ARE GEMINI BORN IN THE YEAR OF THE ROOSTER

### Years of the Rooster

| | | | |
|---|---|---|---|
| 1909 | 1957 | 2005 | 2053 |
| 1921 | 1969 | 2017 | 2065 |
| 1933 | 1981 | 2029 | 2077 |
| 1945 | 1993 | 2041 | 2089 |

Chinese folklore assigns the qualities of sincerity, kindness, and gallantry to the Rooster, and especially honors it as a symbol of courage. The Rooster drives away the dark, bringing clarity and the opportunity to pursue high aspirations. Combine this with your Gemini penchant for saying yes, and it's obvious why you attract success. As a Gemini Rooster, you have impressive skills and swift intelligence and are imbued with an appetite for life. Your wide-ranging interests serve you well professionally, though at times your outspokenness shocks people. It's true you can be self-absorbed and, in emotional situations, unaware of others' hidden agendas. In romantic affairs, you've had your heart broken because you were too trusting. Compatible partners are born in the Years of the Horse, Ox, and Snake.

# IF YOU ARE GEMINI BORN IN THE YEAR OF THE DOG

## Years of the Dog

| | | | |
|------|------|------|------|
| 1910 | 1958 | 2006 | 2054 |
| 1922 | 1970 | 2018 | 2066 |
| 1934 | 1982 | 2030 | 2078 |
| 1946 | 1994 | 2042 | 2090 |

The Year of the Dog always heralds a time of gain through commitment to a goal. In the Asian zodiac, the Dog signifies caring dedication and fierce loyalty—which may seem an uneasy fit with your blasé Gemini attitudes and tendency to flit from subject to subject. However, Dog practicality and industriousness strengthen your Gemini ambition, making you a dynamic go-getter—and all this is wrapped in a witty, entertaining, totally alluring package. As a Gemini Dog, you have a lyrical imagination that you focus on an objective. Plus your talent for close relationships allows you to specialize—you're much less of a dabbler than other Geminis. In love, you give yourself to one person and hold tightly, though you must guard against becoming obsessive and possessive. Compatible partners are born in the Years of the Rabbit, Dog, Pig, and Tiger.

# IF YOU ARE GEMINI BORN IN THE YEAR OF THE PIG

## Years of the Pig

| | | | |
|---|---|---|---|
| 1911 | 1959 | 2007 | 2055 |
| 1923 | 1971 | 2019 | 2067 |
| 1935 | 1983 | 2031 | 2079 |
| 1947 | 1995 | 2043 | 2091 |

The Asian Pig has qualities far superior to those the West assigns. The Pig is chivalrous, intellectual, and extremely capable—and being born in a Pig year shows ability to lead a life of good foundation and successful creative work. Pig determination reinforces your Gemini thinking skills and talent for performing for an audience. As a Gemini Pig, you're expressive, persuasive, ambitious, and a steamroller when you're after a goal. In your work, you light up old ideas and refashion them into ventures that appeal to the public. You have a nose for financial opportunity. Your sweet nature blossoms in friendship and love. You're a passionate nurturer who longs for unconditional love; only when you accept that nothing is perfect will you find true contentment. Compatible partners are born in the Years of the Rabbit, Dog, Pig, and Tiger.

# YOU AND NUMEROLOGY

Numerology is the language of numbers. It is the belief that there is a correlation between numbers and living things, ideas, and concepts. Certainly, numbers surround and infuse our lives (e.g., twenty-four hours in a day, twelve months of the year, etc.). And from ancient times mystics have taught that numbers carry a *vibration*, a deeper meaning that defines how each of us fits into the universe. According to numerology, you are born with a personal number that contains information about who you are and what you need to be happy. This number expresses what numerology calls your life path.

All numbers reduce to one of nine digits, numbers 1 through 9. Your personal number is based on your date of birth. To calculate your number, write your birth date in numerals. As an example, the birth date of May 29, 1984, is written 5-29-1984. Now begin the addition: 5 + 29 + 1 + 9 + 8 + 4 = 56; 56 reduces to 5 + 6 = 11; 11 reduces to 1 + 1 = 2. The personal number for someone born May 29, 1984, is *Two*.

# IF YOU ARE A GEMINI ONE

*Keywords*: Confidence and Creativity

*One* is the number of leadership and new beginnings. You rush into whatever engages your heart—whether a new plan, a love affair, or just finding more pleasure. You're courageous, inventive, and an ambitious optimist. You're attracted to unusual creative pursuits because you like to be one-of-a-kind. You need freedom, for restriction is a psychological prison. Careers you do best in are those in which you communicate to the public and have a lot of independence. As for love, you want ecstasy and passion, and the most exciting part of a flirtation is the beginning.

# IF YOU ARE A GEMINI TWO

*Keywords*: Cooperation and Balance

*Two* is the number of cooperation and creating a secure entity. You are *magnetic*—you attract what you need and gather in. Your magic is not only your people skills, but also your ability to breathe life into empty forms (e.g., a concept, an ambitious business idea, a new relationship) and produce something of worth. You're both creative and practical, and good in careers that combine business and artistry. Unlike many Geminis, you're comfortable showing sensitivity and affection. You're able to make heartfelt connections and are very supportive to those you care for. In love, you're a romantic sensualist.

# IF YOU ARE A GEMINI THREE

*Keywords*: Expression and Sensitivity

*Three* symbolizes self-expression. Being a Three magnifies your Gemini gift for words and your talent for seeing what possibilities exist. You link people together so that they benefit from each other. You stimulate others to think. Because you're a connector, you're much loved as a leader, spokesperson, and friend. In your career, creativity and innovation are your specialties. You're a quick study, mentally active, and are curious about the new. In love you need someone who excites you intellectually and sensually, and understands your complex personality. Casual acquaintances may not see your depth, but in love you must have a soulmate who does.

# IF YOU ARE A GEMINI FOUR

*Keywords*: Stability and Process

*Four* is the number of dedication and loyalty. It represents *foundation*, exactly as a four-sided square does. You like to build, and the direction you go in is up. Gemini has a reputation for being flighty, but you want to create something of value—and you have persistence. Therefore, you're able to accomplish great works. You look for self-expression in your craft, and are at your best when you can go at your own pace without others interfering. Sexually, you're an imaginative and generous lover, and you need a giving and understanding partner with whom you can express your rich sensuality.

## IF YOU ARE A GEMINI FIVE

*Keywords*: Freedom and Discipline

*Five* is the number of change and freedom. You're a gregarious nonconformist. With your chameleon intellect (it can go in any direction) and captivating ability to deal with people, you're a marvelous *persuader*. You charm and influence others, and have power with the public. In friendships, you're quick to jump in to give advice and whatever the other needs. Your deepest desire is to push past boundaries and express your free spirit. This is true sexually, as well, and you are a most inventive lover. But when you give your heart away for keeps it's to someone with whom you passionately mesh—body and mind.

## IF YOU ARE A GEMINI SIX

*Keywords*: Vision and Acceptance

*Six* is the number of teaching, healing, and utilizing your talents. You're geared toward changing the world or at least fixing other people's lives. Being an advice-giver and even a therapist to your friends comes naturally. In addition, you're exacting—especially with yourself. You hold to high standards and bring an artisan's excellence to everything you do. Six carries humanitarian instincts, so you also bring uplifting energy to others. In love, you're fervent about being a helpmate and confidante. You're a true partner as well as a passionate sensualist who gives your all to someone you trust.

## IF YOU ARE A GEMINI SEVEN

*Keywords*: Trust and Openness

*Seven* is the number of the mystic and the intensely focused specialist. You observe and, by analyzing, gain wisdom. You have an instinct for problem-solving, and in a flash understand how things work (in business, between people, etc.). You enjoy communicating your ideas and putting them to use. You're an intellectual and connoisseur of everything creative. You pursue *self*-determination (not being controlled by outside forces). At your core you're extremely loyal and intensely loving, though very selective about relationships. In love, your deepest need is for a partner who can help you in your life's journey.

## IF YOU ARE A GEMINI EIGHT

*Keywords*: Abundance and Power

*Eight* is the number of mastery and authority. You are intelligent, alert, quick in action, born to take control in your own hands and guide traffic in the direction you want. You work well with groups because you see what's needed and can delegate (a major success tool). You're also a good judge of character. Others sense you're the one who knows best, and they're right. As a Gemini Eight, you're likely to reach out to diversified groups, travel, and add to your education. Giving your promise in love is a serious act. You're a protective and caring lover, and in turn you need to know your lover is your loyal ally.

# IF YOU ARE A GEMINI NINE

*Keywords*: Integrity and Wisdom

*Nine* is the path of the "old soul," the number of completion and full bloom. Because it's the last number, it sums up the highs and lows of human experience, and you live a life of dramatic events. People see you as colorful and heroic because you have an adventurous outlook but are also spiritual and altruistic. You're intellectual, interested in all kinds of exploration, do highly original work, and are an inspiration to others. In love, you're truthful and sincere—and also a romantic, sensual creature. As a Gemini Nine you generously give of yourself, often to the point of being sacrificing.

# LAST WORD: YOUR GEMINI UNFINISHED BUSINESS

Psychologists often use the phrase *unfinished business* to describe unresolved issues—for example, patterns from childhood that cause unhappiness, anger that keeps one stuck, or scenarios of family dysfunction that repeat through second and third generations (such as alcoholism or abusive behavior).

Astrology teaches that the past is indeed very much with us in the present—and that using astrological insights can help us move out of emotional darkness into greater clarity. Even within this book (which is not a tome of hundreds of pages) you have read of many of the superlatives and challenges of being Gemini. You have breathtaking gifts, and at the same time certain tendencies that can undermine utilizing these abilities.

In nature, a fascinating fact is that in jungles and forests a poisonous plant will grow in a certain spot, and always just a few feet away is a plant that is the antidote to that specific poison. Likewise, in astrology, the antidote is right there, ready to be used when the negatives threaten to overwhelm your life.

Gemini's unfinished business has to do with the need for *mind control*—controlling your mind that tends to run riot. Gemini suffers from what a client of mine calls her "crazy monkey mind." Your mind is bombarded with thoughts, plans, distractions, imaginings, bits of information, mood swings, and anxiety. You have difficulty finding a clearing in the woods.

High-strung to begin with, you have a mind that can create all kinds of worrisome scenarios. And anything that causes inner anxiety plays havoc with your already overwrought nervous system. Lots of fretting, apprehension, and sleepless nights result. Anxiety fuels your Gemini reluctance and ambivalence, which in turn prevents growth. Your career is affected because your creativity is blocked. All that thinking without coming to a decision allows opportunities to slip away.

A disciplined mind is calm and focused, but a mind out of control just spins you deeper into a psychological hole. Your thinking processes usually override your emotions—generally, you're not in touch with the anger or sadness that can tell you something important. So your mind is likely to be the only means you have of explaining yourself to you. It is most important, therefore, that your mind works for you and not against you.

Inherent in the Gemini experience is the issue of dissipation and waste—wasting time and energy, starting and then abandoning, taking the easy way out and not following through, looking for "freedom." To some degree, freedom to you means not having others looking over your shoulder, assessing your performance, judging you. You're not as confident as you appear. Astrology teaches that in your sign of Gemini the "ego need" is strong but the "ego" is weak—and that your Gemini quest is to find (through the challenges in life you overcome) the strong mind *and* heart that is your birthright.

An important tool for building up your ego is strengthening your self-discipline. Even as freewheeling a Gemini as Bob Dylan is quoted as saying, "A hero is someone who understands the responsibility that comes with his freedom." This is a good paraphrase of what the Buddha teaches: *Freedom and discipline are inseparable.*

On a psychological level, Gemini searches for the other Twin, the strong twin that can supply what you need for completion. Too often Gemini looks to another person for this and has a tendency to become, in convoluted ways, dependent in relationships. Yet you truly have within yourself the other Twin—and this is your *heart.*

Be assured, Gemini, that the antidotes to every one of your difficulties are right there, to be found in their entirety in being Gemini. You're a creator and also a connector to people (as well as being able to connect people to other people). You have scintillating mental energy and one of your greatest antidotes is your willingness to explore. You're an open person, not a closed system. Therefore, you're able to grow in ways others are not. You're made of sterner stuff than you think. You have the capacity to hold fast to a project, an area of expertise, and bring it into bloom in a manner that astounds the public. You have *unexpectedness* to your talents.

You are filled with emotion and passion, and all you have to do is recognize your feelings. To again use the simile of *The Wizard of Oz*, like Dorothy you have always had the power to return home.

Your Gemini unfinished business is also everything you are still on the way to accomplishing. Remember, you're the sign of potential—of embracing change and taking advantage of the moment. How many people are stuck in old ways? You, Gemini, have the power of *now*. You have high intellect, a sunny sense of humor, and awesome communication skills. You're someone truly alive. Love, wisdom, fulfillment, and a secure life that rewards you for your special talents are all yours to gain. These are your unfinished business.

# FAMOUS PEOPLE WITH THE SUN IN GEMINI

Paula Abdul
Tim Allen
F. Lee Bailey
Josephine Baker
Annette Bening
Mel Blanc
George H. W. Bush
Rachel Carson
Rosemary Clooney
Joan Collins
Jacques Cousteau
Mario Cuomo
Tony Curtis
Johnny Depp
Arthur Conan Doyle
Albrecht Dürer
Bob Dylan
Clint Eastwood
Ralph Waldo Emerson
Douglas Fairbanks
Ian Fleming
Errol Flynn
Michael J. Fox
Judy Garland
Paul Gauguin
Lou Gehrig
Allen Ginsberg
Benny Goodman
Steffi Graf
Che Guevara
Nathan Hale
Marvin Hamlisch

Dashiell Hammett
Lillian Hellman
Bob Hope
Gerard Manley Hopkins
Hubert Humphrey
Allen Iverson
Angelina Jolie
Tom Jones
Louis Jourdan
John F. Kennedy
Nicole Kidman
Henry Kissinger
Anna Kournikova
Lenny Kravitz
Hugh Laurie
Peggy Lee
Federico García Lorca
Robert Ludlum
Paul McCartney
Malcolm McDowell
Larry McMurtry
Barry Manilow
Thomas Mann
Dean Martin
Marilyn Monroe
Bill Moyers
Joe Namath
Liam Neeson
Joyce Carol Oates
Jacques Offenbach
Laurence Olivier
Frank Oz

Cole Porter
Prince
Alexander Pushkin
Basil Rathbone
Sally Ride
Joan Rivers
Isabella Rossellini
Henri Rousseau
Salman Rushdie
Marquis de Sade
Jean-Paul Sartre
Maurice Sendak
Tupac Shakur
Brooke Shields
Harriet Beecher Stowe
Richard Strauss
William Styron
Kathleen Turner
Donald Trump
Richard Wagner
Kanye West
Ruth Westheimer
Walt Whitman
Gene Wilder
Hank Williams Jr.
Venus Williams
Herman Wouk
Frank Lloyd Wright
William Butler Yeats

# PART TWO

# ALL ABOUT YOUR SIGN OF GEMINI

# GEMINI'S ASTROLOGICAL AFFINITIES, LINKS, AND LORE

## SYMBOL: The Twins 👥

The Twins are associated with humanism, versatility, communication. In different mythologies, the Twins have been twin siblings (either two brothers, two sisters, or brother and sister) or lovers. The Twins represent duality (between mind and matter, and mind and body) as well as the concept of soulmates.

## RULING PLANET: Mercury ☿

The ancient Roman god was the messenger and go-between. The name Mercury comes from a Latin word meaning "commerce." In Greek mythology, Mercury was known as Hermes, God of the "Persuasive Tongue." In astrology Mercury rules communication, speaking, writing, and reasoning, all forms of exchange of ideas and information, and travel. Its influence emphasizes quick cleverness, dexterity, and a nervous temperament.

# DOMINANT KEYWORD

I THINK

# GLYPH ♊

The pictograph represents the two figures of the Twins. The two upright figures are joined at the head (communication and ideas) and at the feet (their common ground). This is the Roman numeral for 2. Esoteric astrology speaks of the glyph representing the duality between day and night, male and female, conscious and unconscious, earth and heaven. The dual symbol also pictures the human arms or lungs (the parts of the body that Gemini rules). In symbolic terms, two upright lines bounded by top and bottom lines represent wisdom, learning, and the powers of the mind to synthesize information.

# PART OF THE BODY RULED BY GEMINI:
## The Hands, Arms, Shoulders, and Lungs

Geminis are susceptible to strains and accidents involving arms and hands. They are also prone to bronchitis and respiratory ailments.

## LUCKY DAY: Wednesday

The day named for Mercury, ruler of Gemini. "Wednesday" comes from Old Norse words meaning *"Woden's Day"* (Woden was the god associated with Mercury).

## LUCKY NUMBERS: 5 and 9

Numerologically, 5 is the number of adaptability, curiosity, gregariousness, and enthusiasm—and 9 is linked to knowledge, imagination, social skills, and an evolved mind. These qualities align with the nature of Gemini.

## TAROT CARD: The Lovers

The card in the Tarot linked to Gemini is the Lovers. Ancient names for this card are Children of the Voices and Oracle of the Mighty Gods. In the Tarot this card represents love and joining together, and on a deeper level speaks about the challenge of relationships. Its message is to not lose oneself in another person, not to lose one's own identity, and to stay true to oneself. When the Lovers turns up in a Tarot reading, it points to two paths ahead and an important choice that must be made with care and with the heart. In some old Tarot decks, this card is called the Two Paths.

The card itself pictures a nude man and woman who stand beneath the outstretched arms of the Angel Raphael. The man, who is on the right side of the card, looks at the woman on the left of the card—and she looks up at the angel. The man represents intellect and reason (the conscious). The woman represents emotion and feelings (the unconscious). She is the one able to receive guidance from the higher consciousness of the angel.

For Gemini, the Lovers tells you to turn away from your "shadow" self (the bad twin), and you will find the balance between head and heart. It encourages your ability to love and be loved, and to create harmony in your life. It assures you that you have the ability to always make the right decision and be on the right path.

## MAGICAL BIRTHSTONE: Agate

A precious stone characterized by its fine grain, different patterns, brightness, and array of colors. Down through history, the agate was thought to protect the wearer from accidents and falls, and has long been used by seafarers to promote a safe voyage and have a calming effect on storms at sea. In old Europe the stone was set into horses' manes and bridles to keep the rider safe. Certain agates resembling an eye were worn as a protection against the evil eye. It was also believed the gem had the power to attract the favor of God. For Geminis, the agate is said to protect from deception and falsehood and to bestow eloquence, especially in declarations of love.

## SPECIAL COLOR: Yellow

Bright and luminous, the color of novelty and dazzle. Yellow signifies light, truth, the intellect and intuition, and timelessness.

## CONSTELLATION OF GEMINI

From earliest times, this constellation was known as the Twins. (*Gemini* is the Latin word for twins.) The stars in this constellation form a distinct picture of twins—when the stars are connected by lines, the result is a drawing of two human figures holding hands. The brightest stars in this constellation are Castor and Pollux, who in Greek and Roman mythology were twin brothers. In the myth, Castor and Pollux had different fathers (one mortal and one immortal), and the god Zeus, father of Pollux, placed the twin brothers in the heavens as the constellation Gemini so they might be bonded forever as an immortal pair, in constant communication. The Babylonians saw the Twins as the pairing of intellect and intuition.

## CITIES

London, San Francisco, Versailles, Melbourne

## COUNTRIES

United States, Wales, Belgium

## FLOWERS

Lily of the Valley and Lavender

# TREES

Nut-bearing trees

# HERBS AND SPICES

Aniseed, Marjoram, and Caraway

# METAL: Mercury

Named for the god Mercury who governed mobility, speed, and communication. The written symbols for the planet Mercury (ruler of Gemini) and the metal mercury are the same. Mercury is one of only four metals that are liquid at room temperature. In this state mercury is known as "quicksilver," suggestive of something difficult to pin down and the quick-moving quality of thoughts and ideas. Ancient alchemists thought mercury to be symbolic of the soul.

# ANIMALS RULED BY GEMINI

Brightly colored birds and butterflies and the monkey

## DANGER

Gemini people are prone to accidents while traveling. Their fickle natures also tend to arouse unexpected anger in others, the depth of which Geminis often misjudge.

## PERSONAL PROVERB

Progress is not created by contented people.

## KEYWORDS FOR GEMINI

Curious
Independent
Versatile
Communicative
Outgoing
Humorous and entertaining
Adaptable
Needs to know
Creates new ideas
Mercurial, changeable
Easily bored
Nonconformist
High-strung
Cerebral
Clever
Resourceful

Opportunist
Manipulative
A trickster
Detached emotionally
Quirky sex drive (plays mind games with lovers)
Looks for twin soul in a romantic partner

# HOW ASTROLOGY SLICES AND DICES YOUR SIGN OF GEMINI

## DUALITY: Masculine

The twelve astrological signs are divided into two groups, *masculine* and *feminine*. Six are masculine and six are feminine; this is known as the sign's *duality*. A masculine sign is direct and energetic. A feminine sign is receptive and magnetic. These attributes were given to the signs about 2,500 years ago. Today modern astrologers avoid the sexism implicit in these distinctions. A masculine sign does not mean "positive and forceful" any more than a feminine sign means "negative and weak." In modern terminology, the masculine signs, such as your sign of Gemini, are defined as outer-directed and strong through action. The feminine signs are self-contained and strong through inner reserves.

## TRIPLICITY (ELEMENT): Air

The twelve signs are also divided into groups of three signs. Each of these three-sign groups is called a *triplicity*, and each of these denotes an *element*. The elements are *Fire*, *Earth*, *Air*, and *Water*. In astrology, an element symbolizes a fundamental characterization of the sign.

The three *Fire* signs are Aries, Leo, and Sagittarius. Fire signs are active and enthusiastic.

The three *Earth* signs are Taurus, Virgo, and Capricorn. Earth signs are practical and stable.

The three *Air* signs are Gemini, Libra, and Aquarius. Air signs are intellectual and communicative.

The three *Water* signs are Cancer, Scorpio, and Pisces. Water signs are emotional and intuitive.

## QUADRUPLICITY (QUALITY): Mutable

The twelve signs are also divided into groups of four signs. Each of these four-sign groups is called a *quadruplicity*, and each of these denotes a *quality*. The qualities are *Cardinal*, *Fixed*, and *Mutable*. In astrology, the quality signifies the sign's interaction with the outside world.

Four signs are *Cardinal\** signs. These are Aries, Cancer, Libra, and Capricorn. Cardinal signs are enterprising and outgoing. They are the initiators and leaders.

Four signs are *Fixed*. These are Taurus, Leo, Scorpio, and Aquarius. Fixed signs are resistant to change. They are perfectors and finishers, rather than originators.

---

\*When the Sun crosses the four cardinal points in the zodiac, we mark the beginning of each of our four seasons. Aries begins spring; Cancer begins summer; Libra begins fall; Capricorn begins winter.

Four signs are *Mutable*. These are Gemini, Virgo, Sagittarius, and Pisces. Mutable signs are flexible, versatile, and adaptable. They are able to adjust to differing circumstances.

Your sign of Gemini is a Masculine, Air, Mutable sign—and no other sign in the zodiac is this exact combination. Your sign is a one-of-a-kind combination, and therefore you express the characteristics of your duality, element, and quality differently from any other sign.

For example, your sign is a *Masculine* sign, meaning you are energetic and assertive. You're an *Air* sign, meaning you're facile with words and ideas, talented at expressing yourself. And you're a *Mutable* sign, meaning you're able to go with the flow, adjust, and quickly adapt to new situations.

Now, the sign of Libra is also Masculine and Air, but unlike Gemini (which is Mutable), Libra is Cardinal. Therefore, like you, Libra is active and has a lively mind. But Libra is also more conscious of its image. Libra needs attention and approval, and its Cardinal energies are directed toward initiating relationships. Being supported by others gives Libra the freedom to use its Cardinal qualities of inventiveness and communication. Like you, Libra enjoys new learning, but its motivation is to be part of a team and to pursue anything that creates a harmonious environment. Libra isn't as willing as you to give something a try for fear of ending up looking foolish. You, Gemini, are Mutable, which means you're motivated by curiosity. You seek new experiences and develop very versatile talents. You look for intellectual freedom and are less dependent on what other people think. Your Mutable quality makes you able to grasp ideas in a flash and run with them.

Aquarius, too, is Masculine and Air; but unlike Gemini (which is Mutable), Aquarius is Fixed. Aquarius, like you, loves exploring new ideas and approaches life with enthusiasm. However, being Fixed, Aquarius doesn't have your flexibility in playing with ideas and trying variations. When Aquarius forms an opinion or becomes attached to a cause, it stubbornly holds to its way of thinking. It can become known as eccentric and iconoclastic. Aquarius tends to get fixed on the role of the rebel and being different from others. Aquarius can also become obsessively stuck in an unworkable situation, and won't let it go. You, being Mutable, have a mind that moves in many directions and you're unlikely to get bogged down on any one path. Your Mutable restlessness brings you into contact with a variety of people, and you're stimulated by exchanges of opinions. You're far more willing than Aquarius to shift your focus and take a new tack. Certainly, you'll quickly move toward a goal that's doable—and not waste energy on the unproductive.

## POLARITY: Sagittarius

The twelve signs are also divided into groups of two signs. Each of these two-sign groups is called a *polarity* (meaning "opposite"). Each sign in the zodiac has a polarity, which is its opposite sign in the other half of the zodiac. The two signs express opposite characteristics.

Gemini and Sagittarius are a polarity. Gemini is the sign of self-expression, reasoning, delivering information, and communicating on a personal level. You're smart, clever, and quick-witted. You have an eye for detail and are interested in other people. You have a special gift for observing. You notice human behavior, study motivations, and are able to precisely analyze a situation. This makes you adept at spotting opportunity (which adds to your reputation as being a bit of a conniver).

Astrology teaches that Gemini rules "immediate environment," and your activities tend to be with those involved in your day-to-day life. You like ideas that are practical, and are adept at speaking, informing, and negotiating. Gemini is considered a "personal" sign because your energy is focused on interacting with people and fitting yourself into what's at hand. Notwithstanding, you also enjoy trying to impose your point of view on others. Your stock in trade is an iridescent ability to charm and amuse.

Sagittarius, your opposite sign, is the sign of far-flung places and the quest for freedom. Unlike you, who enjoys interrelating with scores of close friends and contacts and loves to sway an audience (e.g., in business or creative work), Sagittarius resists ties that bind and wants to go off traveling (on all levels—emotional, physical, and intellectual). Sagittarius is born with wanderlust and moves with the winds of change. The sign of Sagittarius is associated with higher learning, expansion, long journeys, and foreign lands. The Sagittarius drive aspires to something with greater meaning. It wants to rise above the petty and aim toward a loftier calling. Natives of this sign are spurred by a sense of mission (many focus on causes or political activism), and try not to get tied down with personal commitments. Sagittarius is not at home in the minutiae of ordinary life; its energy comes alive when leaping toward a new horizon.

Astrologically, you as a Gemini can benefit from adopting some of Sagittarius's desire to stay above the fray and apart from the crowd. Sagittarius is generous and can be kind and sympathetic to others, but does not easily become involved. Cerebral as you are, Gemini, you're also people-oriented and are fond of dispensing advice (you're a *communicator*). But your life would run smoother if you incorporated some of Sagittarius's ability not to get enmeshed in complicated relationships that you keep trying to fix. You need to practice detachment from petty people and set your sights on expansive goals for yourself. While Gemini's attention is on improving and rearranging, Sagittarius's is on personal liberation and widening its horizons.

In turn, Sagittarius has much to learn from you, and at the top of this list is forming connections. Among your best qualities is your willingness to jump in to bring cheer and support. You have strong links to your immediate environment of friendships, acquaintances, and social life that fulfill you. Sagittarius struggles with conflict around closeness, and its no-strings attitude can be isolating. Sagittarius can also benefit from learning from you how to live in the now. Sagittarius is future-oriented, and one of its pitfalls is wasting time, energy, and brainpower on unrealistic pursuits. Your Gemini magic emanates from your immediacy—from your involvement in life as it unfolds around you.